POCKET IMAGES

Reading

POCKET IMAGES

Reading

Peter Southerton

NONSUCH

BERKSHIRE BOOKS

First published 1992
This new pocket edition 2007
Images unchanged from first edition

Nonsuch Publishing Limited
Cirencester Road, Chalford
Stroud, Gloucestershire, GL6 8PE
www.nonsuch-publishing.com

Nonsuch Publishing is an imprint of NPI Media Group

British Library Cataloguing in Publication Data.
A catalogue record for this book is available from the British Library.

ISBN 978-1-84588-426-0

Typesetting and origination by NPI Media Group
Printed in Great Britain

Contents

Introduction

A companion volume to Reading in Old Photographs, published in 1988, this second selection of photographs, some old and others of more recent date, takes the reader through the streets of the town to view some of the changes that have taken place over the years since Queen Victoria's reign. It is hoped this volume will prove as enjoyable and nostalgic an excursion for established residents of the town, to whom it is dedicated, and a further source of interest to those familiar only with Reading as it is today but who would like to know more of what has gone before.

A photograph can tell us a great deal about the people of an earlier generation and about places that have gone through the process of change. In common with the majority of prosperous urban communities in the region, the pace of change in Reading since the Second World War has been relentless. Large companies that were once synonymous with Reading and upon which a considerable proportion of the community once relied for their livelihood have been exchanged for businesses whose processes, premises and patterns of employment are completely different. It is necessary for an example only to point to the makers of electronic equipment, the providers of consumer services and the major finance houses that now occupy the site of Huntley & Palmers once huge factory. Likewise, whole neighbourhoods that, in the not too distant past, were cohesive communities have been uprooted and their residents dispersed, albeit to more salubrious surroundings.

The story of Reading's growth is too well known to be repeated at any length in these pages. It is sufficient to say that it began as a tiny settlement close to the Best ford on the lower reaches of the Kennet. Real growth began with the establishment of the great Benedictine Abbey, the richest in the land, which for more than four centuries was to flourish as a centre of pilgrimage and worship and from time to time even as the seat of government. Even before Henry VIII had decreed the dissolution of the religious houses, the town was a centre for the manufacture and sale of woollen cloth, with merchants coming from afar to do business at the fairs and markets. The civil and economic disruption caused by the Civil War and a decline in the cloth trade brought unemployment and hardship, and for a while the town's fortunes were in eclipse. Before long, however, its favourable situation as regards roads and waterways brought revival. The Rivers Kennet and Thames had for long provided a vital route to the capital for the goods from its markets.

The improvement in the eighteenth century of the principal highways made the carriage of goods easier and travel by coach more agreeable. The cutting of the Kennet and Avon Canal to provide a waterway to Bristol attracted new trades and industries. The wealth thus generated brought about a considerable increase in the population of the borough. The completion in 1840 of the Great Western Railway contributed to the demise of the canal, but Reading became an important railway centre. As travel became easier and the cost of carriage of goods fell, local products, including Suttons seeds, Huntley & Palmers biscuits and Simonds' ales, gained for the town a worldwide reputation for quality. By the end of the century, Reading had changed from a town dependent on agriculture to a busy and rather grimy centre of commerce. While 'beer, bulbs and biscuits' were predominant, there was a growing variety of other manufacturing industries to be found there. As more people were attracted to the area the residential quarters of the town expanded rapidly; pleasant areas were laid out for more prosperous residents, new town houses built in local brick for the middle classes, and row upon row of modest terrace dwellings erected for the workers. The commercial prosperity of the town, the enterprise and philanthropy of many of its leading citizens, and positive action on the part of the Corporation resulted in great improvements to local amenities, although in some instances the heritage of former ages was cast aside rather thoughtlessly to make room for the new. Progress and change continued at a steady pace until the end of the Second World War. Thereafter, the face of the town changed so rapidly that people returning after only a few years absence were heard to complain that they could hardly recognize it. A few familiar landmarks are still to be found but a great many have disappeared. The expanding town has swallowed up villages such as Woodley and Earley which were once considered to be quite separate, while local government rehousing projects and private development in other areas have spilled over into what was, a short while ago, good agricultural land. In spite of all, Reading remains a lively and interesting place in which to live.

One

Town Views

Broad Street in Edwardian days.

The minster church of St Mary is regarded as the mother church of Reading. A Christian church is believed to have existed on this spot long before the Norman Conquest. Rebuilt in the sixteenth century, the fabric incorporates stone and timbers from the former abbey. The decorative cross erected by the parishioners of St Mary's commemorates Isaac Harrinson, a local surgeon, who contributed generously towards the improvement of the area.

Old cottages in the Butts, 1886. Far from being the tidy thoroughfare that it is today, the Butts was until the middle of the last century lined with small, very old houses, some of wattle-and-daub construction. A row of small cottages also stood where the central traffic island is now situated.

Clearance and reconstruction around the church, 1886. To improve the area the tumbledown buildings which had for centuries surrounded the church were pulled down.

St Mary's Butts, looking northwards towards West Street and Greyfriars church, c. 1909. St Mary's churchyard has been considerably enlarged by the removal of the old cottages by which it was surrounded. Public conveniences are now situated where another row of decaying cottages once stood. The coffee stall set up at that time by the Reading Temperance Society flourishes to the present day.

16322   CROSS STREET
(FROM BROAD STREET)
IN 1886

READING.

OLDE CURIOSITY SHOPPE.

ANTIQUE FURNITURE. CHINA,
PICTURE, & WORKS OF ART STORES.

24   THOMAS FLEMING'S   24

CYDER

WINE & SPIRIT
MERCHANT

In festive mood for the coronation of King Edward VII, 1902. Wellsteeds have put out the flags and decorations. A prosperous concern, this drapers was the first shop in the street to install plate-glass windows. Next door, not overshadowed by his neighbour's patriotic fervour, André Monod, Swiss pastry cook and proprietor of the Helvetia Tea Rooms, also displays his national flag.

Opposite above: Broad Street in the 1870s. The town's principal thoroughfare was transformed by the removal in 1862 of Middle Row, Butcher Row and Fisher Row which had formerly obstructed its eastern end. The street is lined with a variety of shops and boasts eleven public houses and two breweries. On the left is Ferguson's Brewery, built on the site of the ancient Angel coaching inn. To the right at the corner of Cross Street is the Bull Inn. The rails of the Reading Tramway Company have yet to be laid.

Opposite below: Cross Street from Broad Street, 1886. The Bull Inn has been rebuilt, while Ye Olde Curiosity Shoppe stands shuttered and empty, soon to be pulled down to make way for the Capital and Counties Bank, now a branch of Lloyds Bank plc.

Broad Street viewed from an upper floor window at the corner of Queen Victoria Street, 1905. Cab horses at the rank in the middle of the street stand patiently awaiting their fares and an electric tram sets off in the direction of Wokingham Road.

Broad Street from the junction with West Street in the 1920s. Although the traffic is fairly light, the presence of a policeman on point duty is necessary as the tram routes from west to east Reading and from Caversham Bridge to Whitley cross at this point.

A rare photograph of Reading in wartime. An ordinary day in 1945 and life carries on as usual. The town is fortunate in that little damage has been caused by enemy action. Although the tide of war is at last on the turn, there are many indications that wartime regulations remain in force. As a precaution against attack from the air, the headlamps of the various motor vehicles are masked or obscured, while the white painted bands on the trolley bus standards and the white lines along the centre of the road are for safety in the blackout. The delivery lorry in the foreground carries official marks identifying it as an essential road user. The camouflage-painted vehicle parked a short distance behind belongs to the Ministry of Aircraft Production. Although the last trams were withdrawn from service in May 1939, to be replaced by trolleybuses, the rails remain in place, posing a considerable hazard for cyclists.

Union Street, 1910. The passageway with its central gutter and crowded shops preserves a medieval atmosphere. Known affectionately as Smelly Alley, Union Street is the last of the many courts and alleys which once ran between Broad Street and Friar Street.

Broad Street in the early 1950s. The amount of motor traffic has increased considerably since the Second World War. Traffic flows quite freely, however, and there are few restrictions on kerbside parking. To the left is Woolworth's familiar red and gold fascia. A little further along is Bull's, still a major department store but destined to close in 1953.

West Street, c. 1910. This was a busy shopping area with a pub on each corner. The gabled building next to the Fox Inn is one of Marks & Spencers' two Reading stores opened in 1904. The Vine on the opposite corner was pulled down in the mid-1930s to be replaced by Montague Burton's tailors shop. The row of shops on the right-hand side built by Councillor Fidler at the turn of the twentieth century still survives. At the far end is Greyfriars church.

Friar Street, looking eastwards from the corner of Greyfriars Road, c. 1900. The tall building just left of centre is Blagrave Flats, an early development of its kind. Opposite stands Fidler's Seed Establishment and the Royal County Theatre with its projecting glass verandah.

Friar Street in the late 1930s. To keep the traffic flowing at this busy junction where Station Road and Queen Victoria Street cross, Reading's earliest traffic lights have been installed. Except for the Westminster Bank on the corner and the ivy-clad building next door, this part of Friar Street appears much as it does today.

Friar Street in the early twentieth century. The Queen's Hotel on the left was popular as a family hotel. Being conveniently situated in the centre of the town and offering stock rooms for the display of goods, it was also much frequented by visiting commercial travellers.

Friar Street, 1924. The uncharacteristic emptiness of the street suggests that it is Sunday. The Queen's Hotel has been replaced by the General Post Office, a light and airy building incorporating every refinement to help speed the mail on its way.

Designed by Alfred Waterhouse and opened in 1876, the Municipal Buildings and Town Hall reflected Reading's civic pride. They provided a spacious and ornate council chamber and offices for the growing number of staff required for local government. The original eighteenth-century Assembly Rooms were incorporated in the new building to form the Small Town Hall. Between the Civic Offices and St Laurence's church are the offices of Blandy & Blandy, solicitors, destroyed by enemy action in 1943.

To celebrate Queen Victoria's Diamond Jubilee her statue was erected near the entrance to the Town Hall. Due to the temporary loss of the marble block on its way from Carrara, the work had to be completed by the sculptor, George Blackall Simonds, in record time in order to be ready for the unveiling by the Duke of Cambridge on 27 July 1897.

MARKET PLACE.   1900-01.   READING.

From Mr. & Mrs. John K. Cook, Bank, Reading.

The Market Place on a warm spring day is depicted on this unusual Christmas card for 1900. Many of the old buildings which at that time lined the eastern side, including the Elephant Hotel and Suttons, have disappeared, but the complete redevelopment of the area was halted in the 1960s thanks to the efforts of the newly formed Reading Civic Society.

The corner of King's Road and Duke Street await redevelopment. Lost in the rebuilding were some fine ornamental brickwork and decorative terracotta by Colliers of Tilehurst.

The Old Borough Police Station, High Bridge House. Formed in 1836, the Borough's police force retained its independence until its amalgamation into the Thames Valley Police in 1968. The police station, which was situated initially in Friar Street and later in the Forbury, moved in 1862 to premises adjacent to High Bridge. The building also housed the local Police and Coroner's Courts, while the town's manual fire engine was kept in a shed at the rear. When in 1912 the police moved to larger premises in Valpy Street, the old building was used to accommodate a variety of official and local government offices. By the 1970s, however, it had become increasingly unsound and was in danger of demolition. To save something of this relic of old Reading, the exterior was preserved while the interior was completely rebuilt to be let as business premises.

Medieval cottages in Silver Street, 1887. These buildings were even at this time lacking amenities and in a sad state of repair.

Slum clearance, 1925. 'The rats fled in droves', said a contemporary observer of the demolition of the old Silver Street cottages in 1925. The site is now occupied by old people's flats.

Southampton Street, 1887. Although this is the principal route into the town from Winchester and the South, there is remarkably little traffic and few pedestrians to be seen on this sunny afternoon.

Whitley pump. This old iron pump once supplied the needs of the village of Whitley. It was replaced in the 1850s by a trough fed with piped water for the benefit of horses that were thirsty after hauling their loads up the steep slopes from the town.

Victoria Gate, before the erection of the War Memorial, in the early 1920s. This was the principal entrance to Forbury Gardens. Just to the right of centre is Shire Hall, the offices since 1911 of the Berkshire County Council. Behind the distinctive rounded fascia is Suttons' stables. Both the stables and the fine late seventeenth-century house adjacent were demolished in 1962. The Prudential Assurance Company's offices now occupy the site.

Abbots Walk, looking towards the Forbury and St Laurence's, *c.* 1920. Built in the 1850s as private residences for well-to-do tradesmen, many of these houses were later used by the County Council as offices. All but two have since been demolished to make way for office development.

Reading Abbey. Only fragments remain of the twelfth-century abbey which in its time was the richest and most powerful in the kingdom. Following the dissolution of the religious houses the building was stripped of all valuable materials. Until well into the nineteenth century it was regarded as a free quarry for stone and rubble.

Chestnut Walk. This is a pleasant canalside walk running incongruously beneath the walls of Reading Gaol. The area was once a busy quay. In the 1840s, much of the material used to build the gaol was unloaded here. The corner turrets of the prison, once warders' quarters, were demolished when the building was modernized in 1970.

The Royal Berkshire Hospital, c. 1918. Built in 1839 on land given by Viscount Sidmouth with money raised by public subscription, this hospital originally accommodated eighty patients. The central section with its imposing Ionic portico was the work of the architect Henry Briant. The wings, in similar style, were added in 1881.

During the First World War, wounded servicemen were treated at the Royal Berkshire Hospital as well as in various military-run hospitals in the area. The precise date of this interior view is uncertain, but the proliferation of Union Jacks in the decorations suggests a national celebration, possibly the Armistice.

Left: Totally teetotal, the Lodge Hotel, King's Road. Situated within sight of Huntley & Palmers, this temperance hotel was approved accommodation for travellers and other visitors to the factory.

Below: London Road, looking westwards from Cemetery Junction, 1910. A horse trough stands where the Jack o' Both Sides was later built. Behind the trees of this quiet residential road stand the substantial houses of some of the town's leading professional people, including doctors and surgeons practising at the Royal Berkshire Hospital.

Junction of King's Road and London Road, Reading.

Cemetery Junction, 1908. As the number of people living in the eastern part of Reading increased, a busy shopping area grew up where London Road, King's Road and Wokingham Road converge. On the right, standing head and shoulders above the other buildings, is the Reading Industrial Co-operative Society's new department store with its imposing clock-tower.

Tram Terminus, Wokingham Road — Reading.

The tram terminus, Wokingham Road. The trams on this line gave way to trolleybuses on 20 May 1939.

St Mary's chapel and the Sun Inn. The chapel, which dates from 1798, came into being as a result of divisions within the congregation of St Giles. Built to seat a thousand, the new church occupies the site of the former County Gaol. It is adjacent to the Sun Inn which is probably the oldest of Reading's inns and once supplied refreshment for the felons held in the gaol.

The changing face of Castle Street, 1968. With the development of the new Civic Centre, the north side of Castle Street from the Sun Inn to Howard Street was cleared for the building of the Police HQ and Magistrates Courts. With the demolition disappeared an extensive neighbourhood shopping area.

Sandwiched between Castle Street and Berkeley Avenue, Coley was, until the 1950s, peopled mainly by workers in the larger industrial concerns. It was in essence a nineteenth-century population crammed into the smallest possible space. Despite the preponderance of slum dwellings, a noticeable characteristic of the area was its close-knit sense of community.

Coley in the early 1960s. By this time the greater part of the area had been cleared to make way for the Inner Distribution Road.

The Blue Lion and the Borough Arms, two of Coley's many licensed premises. For many Coleyites the pubs provided warmth and light, and a place where at the weekend their cares and frustrations could be drowned in the cup that both cheers and inebriates. The pubs also played an important role as a leisure centre, providing a meeting place for all kinds of social and political groups, sporting activities and savings clubs.

Coley Park housing estate, 1959. A shortage of land and the increasing cost of conventional two-storey houses and bungalows caused the Council to say, 'if we can't go outwards then we have got to go upwards'. In co-operation with George Wimpey & Co., three blocks of flats, each of fifteen storeys and 135 ft high, were built. The highest buildings in the region to that date, they were hailed by the Council as its 'latest and greatest venture'.

Coley Avenue, its gates surmounted by Wyverns, was once a tree-lined drive leading from Tilehurst Road to the eighteenth-century Coley Park House. Throughout the nineteenth century this was the the home of the Monck family who served Reading well as Members of Parliament and Justices of the Peace. The gates were demolished in 1967.

Bath Road & Prospect Park, Reading

Bath Road, dusty and white, 1903. With the coming of the railway in 1840, and the abolition of the turnpike trusts, the road to Bath, regarded during the eighteenth century as the finest in England, reverted to little more than a rural highway. So it was to remain until the coming of the motor car made its improvement essential.

Maypole Corner, where West Street meets Oxford Road, in the 1920s. The old Fox Inn has recently been acquired by Maypole Stores, a chain store dealing in dairy produce and groceries, which has converted the building for use as a shop.

Oxford Road Methodist church as originally built. The present church was built on the same site in 1893, the foundation stones being laid in March of that year. Boston House to the left and the Manse to the right remain virtually unaltered to the present day.

Russell Street looking towards Holy Trinity church, 1846. The long terrace of comfortable middle-class houses appears much as it does today. This photograph is, however, unusual in that it is one of the earliest of a number of local scenes captured by the lens of William Fox Talbot. A founding father of the science of photography, he developed the 'calotype' process whereby a translucent negative of waxed paper could be used to produce positive images. It was in nearby Russell Terrace, now Baker Street, that the inventor established his Reading Photographic Establishment. Here he produced the world's first photographically illustrated book, *The Pencil of Nature*.

St Andrew's Home, Wilton Road. Established in 1902 by the Church of England Waifs and Strays Society, this children's home, offering a home for thirty-nine orphaned or homeless boys up to the age of fourteen years, is typical of its kind. The boys attended local schools and links with the local community were encouraged.

St Andrew's Home had extensive grounds for sport and play. When in the 1960s changing patterns in child care favoured smaller residential units, the home closed. The house is today used as a welfare centre, while sheltered flats for retired people have been built in the grounds.

Holy Trinity church, 1910. Built in 1826, to serve the gentry who were beginning to establish themselves in properties in the west of the town, this church is unusual in that it has catacombs beneath the nave for use as family vaults. These are not all occupied as legislation forbidding intramural burial came into effect in the 1950s.

Floods in the Oxford Road. Following heavy rain, floods were common in this area in the earlier part of the twentieth century, disrupting the traffic. Armed with his broom, a shopkeeper attempts to repel the waters.

The long-awaited second bridge. When opened in 1923, Reading Bridge was the largest single-span arch of ferro-concrete in the United Kingdom. The old contrasting with the new, a traditional shallow-draft Thames barge passes under the new bridge to moor at the towpath.

Caversham Bridge. When Reading's boundaries were extended in 1911 to take in Caversham, it was stipulated that the existing bridge must be rebuilt or widened. The old iron bridge was replaced by a ferro-concrete structure of two flat arches joined by a single abutment. The new bridge was opened in 1926 having taken two years to complete.

Reading from the air, *c.* 1920. At this time Reading was very much an industrial town. Viewed from above, a variety of industrial premises are clearly visible at the junction of London Road and London Street. Bottom left is Huntley, Boorne & Stevens factory stretching the full length of Crown Street. Immediately behind stands Burbery's Mill Lane factory faced by the Corporation Tramways depot and power station. Wharves and timberyards line the banks of the Kennet. Suttons and Huntley & Palmers extensive factories can be seen in the middle distance, while behind the railway line are visible the chimneys of the factories on the south bank of the Thames.

Two

Trade and Industry

Huntley & Palmers factory from the air, *c.* 1925. At the turn of the twentieth century this factory, which employed almost a quarter of the town's entire labour force, was described as 'a town within a town'.

Working dress (industrial). Stokers at Reading Gasworks, c. 1900. Working in hot and grimy conditions, these men are wearing shirts of heavy material in various colours, trousers of moleskin or corduroy tied below the knee, and iron-shod clogs. As befits his status, the foreman (far right) wears a three-piece suit with muffler and billycock hat.

Working dress (domestic). Stable staff of a large household, c. 1913. At this time, upper- and middle-class families still employed a number of male servants. In this group the head groom (centre) sits between the under groom and coachman. Although they wear no formal uniform, a hat was regarded as essential. A flat cap was favoured by the working man who, as he advanced in seniority, would progress to a bowler.

The Abbey Mill. A water mill to produce flour for the use of Reading Abbey was built beside the Holy Brook in the twelfth century. There was a working mill on the site continuously from that time until 1964 when the last, run by the Soundy family since the mid-nineteenth century, ceased business and a block of County Council offices was erected in its place. During the course of demolition the remains of two Norman arches, a relic of the original mill, were discovered embedded within the fabric of the building. One of the arches has been preserved. It is said that one of the departmental heads, who was to have his office in the new building, objected to having the exposed waterwheels outside his window. The result was that this relic of industrial history was disposed of as scrap.

The mill, after it had ceased to operate, in the early 1980s. A strictly functional Victorian industrial building, its external chutes and ventilators in brick, metal and wood lend a certain grandeur.

The waterwheels which once harnessed the waters of the Holy Brook to power the mill lie exposed and awaiting removal.

Huntley & Palmers factory. As biscuits grew in popularity during the nineteenth century, Huntley & Palmers flourished. By 1914, more than five thousand people were employed at the King's Road factory producing some twenty-five thousand tons of biscuits and cakes annually. Women production workers are leaving for home at the end of the day. Company rules required that male and female workers should leave the factory at different times.

The last days of a giant. When administrative procedures were streamlined in the 1930s, the Victorian office buildings fronting King's Road were replaced by a modern block built by Costains in steel and reinforced concrete. Baking ceased in 1976. By 1990 the whole area had been cleared for redevelopment, the last part to go being the office block.

Inside the 'biscuit city'. Extending from King's Road, across the Kennet to the main Great Western Railway line, the various departments of Huntley & Palmers factory were linked by a maze of bridges, walkways and conveyors. Here the high-level bridge crosses the canal which separates the north and south factory areas. In the background is one of the many oil tanks which fuelled the rows of ovens of the large bakeries.

Bird's Eye View of Messrs. Sutton and Son's Establishment,

Suttons Seeds. Founded in 1807 by John Sutton, the firm expanded to become the largest supplier of garden and vegetable seeds in the country, if not the world. By the end of the nineteenth century the seed stores, packing departments, stables and offices covered an area of six acres, extending from the Market Place to King's Road, Abbey Square and the Forbury. When the company moved to Torquay in 1976, the entire complex was replaced by offices.

Suttons Trial Grounds, London Road. To maintain quality and reliability, all of Suttons seeds were tested at the firm's trial grounds. A feature of the area was the central pavilion where customers were welcome to see for themselves the plants under cultivation. The grounds are now the site of an industrial estate.

Simonds' Brewery (later Courage's) stood beside the Kennet from 1790 until moving to Worton Grange in 1980. The bridge over Southampton Street was for many years a well-known landmark to travellers from Basingstoke and the South.

The Merry Maidens, Shinfield Road, c. 1920. This public house bearing Simonds' hopleaf logo was at this time a small country inn. When later rebuilt, the figures of the legendary Maidens were preserved and installed as a feature of the new building.

The Sun Inn, Castle Street, *c.* 1920. A coaching inn until the coming of the railway, it continued to offer accommodation and stabling until well into the twentieth century.

Ye Olde Boar's Head, Friar Street, 1926. This genuine old town centre inn, which until the 1930s advertised 'very extensive stabling, coach houses and large yard', was used by a number of local carriers as their starting place and in earlier years was the meeting place of Reading's volunteer fire brigade.

Cocks Reading Sauce factory. The sauce was a savoury concoction similar in flavour to Worcester sauce. It remained a household favourite in England and overseas for more than a century. The recipe was devised by William Cocks in 1789 and manufactured at his factory in King's Road. Prepared in steam-heated vessels, the sauce was bottled by hand. It is said that one could locate the premises merely by following one's nose. The factory was demolished in 1985, offices being built on the site.

READING SAUCE,
For Fish, Enriching Gravies &c.
PREPARED AND SOLD
WHOLESALE AND RETAIL
BY the PROPRIETOR,
READING.

This Sauce is generally used at Table with all sorts of Fish, in preference to all other Fish Sauces, and is esteemed peculiarly delicious with Game, Wild Fowl, Hashes, Rump Steaks and Cold Meat.

The distinctive orange label made the sauce easily recognizable on grocers' shelves. James Cocks guarded both the recipe and the design jealously and was never slow to take action against anyone infringing his trademark.

Right: Little Miss Muffet was the trade name of Christopher Hansen's best known product, junket. Established in 1916, the company produced a range of goods connected with milk and dairy products. From small beginnings in Queen's Road, the company expanded in 1934 to larger premises in London Street where it remained until 1957.

Below: Bottling and packing Little Miss Muffet products. At this time most of the processes within the factory were carried out by hand by a large staff of women and girls.

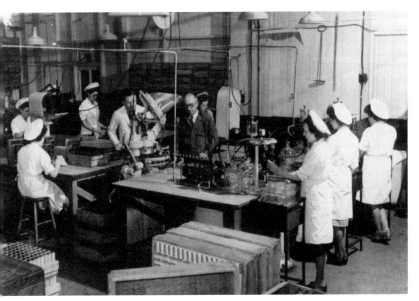

The new Little Miss Muffet factory takes shape, 1957. The company transferred from its town centre site to purpose-built premises, here in the course of construction, in the town's expanding light industrial area to the west of Basingstoke Road.

Celebrating Little Miss Muffet's Golden Jubilee, 1966. The staff are outside the factory, shortly before enjoying a celebratory dinner.

Canning fruit at the CWS preserve factory, 1947. Built in 1919 on land between the Kennet and Elgar Road, the Co-operative Wholesale Society's preserve factory supplied co-operative stores across the country with 'own brand' jams, tinned fruit and pickles. The factory's operations were labour intensive and employed large numbers of local men and women.

The Reading and Caversham Laundry, 1902. By the end of the nineteenth century, laundry work, once the preserve of women who made a living by taking in washing, was increasingly being undertaken by the mechanized 'steam laundries'.

The Cattle Market, Great Knollys Street, 1934. The Mayor of Reading, Cllr William Bale, is officiating at the opening of the new sales ring. Behind him on his left is Lumley Thimbleby, and in the white coat is John Kirkwood. Both were partners in the firm of Thimbleby & Shorland, chartered auctioneers, prominent for over sixty years in the sale of Dairy Shorthorn cattle.

An outdoor cattle sale, March 1947. A rapid thaw following a prolonged period of snow and frost caused severe flooding in Reading and Lower Caversham. Flood water having invaded the market, the March sale of Shorthorn cattle took place in Great Knollys Street.

E.V. Mundy, butcher and poulterer, of Oxford Road, 1934. Mundy and his staff present a fine display of meat and poultry for Christmas.

W.J. Stevens, fishmongers and butchers shops, Oxford Road. The display of meat and fish for sale, unrefrigerated and exposed to the open air, is now strictly forbidden by food hygiene regulations.

The neighbourhood shop, c. 1910. Until well after the Second World War, every residential neighbourhood had its modest general store. This was usually open at all hours and offered everything from cups through candles and biscuits to bootlaces. A shop could be set up for little cost, but to succeed the shopkeeper needed to be a prodigiously hard worker with an acute business sense. Typical of its kind is this family-owned business in Coley.

Prospect Street, Caversham. Bread, cakes and dainties of all kinds were baked on the premises and sold by the Misses Talbot at their shop in Prospect Street. This is now the premises of the Caversham Bookshop.

Duke Street, 1909. His calling advertised by the traditional apothecary's jars prominent in his window, John Rowell, 'Chymist', assisted by his staff of 'Qualified Chymists', dispensed medicines on prescription and sold all manner of pills, ointments and mixtures of his own making.

B   17

Thomas Waite's pianoforte and music warehouse, Duke Street, 1909. Waite poses for the camera as two of his porters prepare to load an upright model into the delivery van. The small frontage of the shop is deceptive, as it extended through into King's Road and displayed not only pianos but a wide variety of other musical instruments.

The Reading Dairy Company shop, Oxford Road, *c.* 1890. 'Pure milk delivered to all parts daily', the sign in the window announces. These rather dismal premises were soon to be removed and the road widened. The demolition work appears already to have begun.

Street traders, 1946. Housewives cluster around a vegetable cart in Wolseley Street, while a milkman with his three-wheeled 'pram' delivers to the doorstep. Not only did street traders with a regular round save the housewife a journey to the shops, but they were cheaper on account of their smaller overheads.

Queuing for oranges, 1947. When imported fruit reappeared in the shops after the Second World War it was greatly in demand. Hitherto a luxury available only to favoured customers, the first oranges to be openly sold in the market attracted long queues of eager shoppers.

The art of window dressing. Many shopkeepers felt that the more goods that could be displayed in their windows the better. McIllroy's Oxford Road department store was no exception.

Heelas, Broad Street, 1934. Although the window dressing of some department stores was more restrained, displays were still used to show the items on sale rather than as a means of tempting prospective purchasers into the shop.

A.H. Bull's drapery store, Broad Street, shortly after the war. Clothes rationing is still in force, but customers are reminded that only one coupon is required for four handkerchieves.

Wall's carnival stores, Caversham Road, in the 1930s. Fancy dress costumes, masks, games, trick sausages, jumping beans and 'the latest crash-bangs' are all on sale. This store continues to the present day to fascinate and delight children of all ages.

The Reading Industrial Co-operative Society combined its head office and department store in new premises in West Street and Cheapside in 1928. Until this time the society had branches in all parts of the town but no effective town centre 'flagship'. The new store had three sales floors served by lifts, a branch of the Co-op Bank, a restaurant, and an assembly hall for meetings and public performances.

To provide additional window space, a covered arcade ran from West Street to Cheapside.

The first Broad Street store of Woolworths. The Woolworth chain of high street shops attracted custom by offering a wide range of lines at a fixed price of 3d or 6d. This store opened in 1923, moving to larger premises extending from Broad Street through to Friar Street in 1939. During the 1960s the premises further expanded to open onto West Street.

Walsingham House at the corner of Broad Street and Minster Street. This was one of Reading's truly old houses. It was the home of Reading's own motor car, the Speedwell, two of which are parked outside the showroom. The Speedwell car went out of production in about 1905 and the building was demolished soon after.

The Speedwell motor car of 1903. It can at least be said that the driver of this two-seater had a good view of the road ahead.

Herbert Engineering of Caversham, with a range of H.E. cars lined up outside the Wolsey Road works. The company began by building gearboxes for Thorneycrofts of Basingstoke. Motor car production commenced in 1919.

War work at Herbert Engineering. In 1916 the company won a valuable contract to repair Le Rhone & Clergot rotary aero engines. The machine shop was greatly enlarged and at one time some seven hundred men were employed, working day and night.

A row of aero engines receiving attention. While the factory did not have a moving assembly line, work there was carried out in a well-regulated and methodical way.

With the return of peace and no more aero engines to repair, the company changed to motor engineering, favouring high-quality sports cars. Among their earlier models was the 13.9 horse power 14/20, based on the Italian Bugatti.

A very successful vehicle was this light car of 11.9 horse power. Not only did it prove itself in hill-climb events, but in 1921, driven at Brooklands by a Mr Sully, it established a record in the flying half-mile of 87.3 m.p.h.

H.E. also produced a range of saloon cars and tourers. The meticulous attention paid to detail meant that few cars were produced. Profits were in consequence small and financial difficulties followed. The company went into receivership in 1924. It was reconstructed and continued in business until 1931.

Sigmund Pulsometer Pumps Ltd. This company moved to Reading from London in 1901 and established its factory on the very edge of the town at a time when Oxford Road was little more than a country lane. Its principal product, the Pulsometer Pump, was to gain for the company a worldwide reputation for craftsmanship and quality.

The Foundry, Pulsometer Pumps factory, 1945. Under the eye of a skilled foreman, molten steel is poured into sand-lined moulds, a hot, heavy and dangerous task.

Aircraft production at Woodley. The firm of Phillips & Powis, manufacturers of pedal and motorcycles, started building light aircraft at their workshops at Woodley Aerodrome from about 1928. They were joined in 1932 by F.G. Miles, a designer whose monoplanes proved an instant success, and the company was soon regarded as one of the country's leading manufacturers of light aircraft. In 1938 when the Second World War was imminent, the company won the largest contract ever to be granted by the Air Ministry to build training aircraft, including the famous Miles Magister. The factory expanded and at the peak of its wartime activity employed some seven thousand workers. To meet production targets a continuous production line was developed in which every conceivable kind of equipment, including surplus Reading Corporation tramlines and electrical components, was pressed into service. In 1943 the firm was renamed Miles Aircraft Ltd, after its famous designer. After the Second World War the company experienced hard times and finally went into liquidation. Handley Page continued to build aircraft at Woodley until 1962, when the once busy airfield was redeveloped as a modern light industrial and housing area.

Portable milking equipment under test, 1946. Mr George H. Gascoigne was already in his fifties when, with his wife as secretary and a staff of three, he established a company to market Kee Klamps, tubular joints for agricultural use. Their first premises were in two rooms over a shop in the Market Place. There followed a move to premises near the Cattle Market and then, in August 1939, to a three acre factory site in Berkeley Avenue. By this time the company was engaged in the development and manufacture of dairy equipment, work of vital importance during the war years.

Caversham Park. In the course of its long history, this estate has had many wealthy owners. Following a disastrous fire in 1850, the house, then the home of the Crawshay family, prosperous ironmasters of South Wales, was completely rebuilt and decorated in Italian style, no expense being spared. In 1922 the house and much of the estate was acquired by the Oratory School whose pupils were to enjoy these very fine surroundings until moving to their present home at Woodcote shortly before the outbreak of the Second World War.

The lavish nature of the interior of the house at Caversham Park was not diminished by its use as a school. It was indeed a suitable setting for an educational establishment, having been founded in 1859 by Cardinal Newman for 'Catholics of the Upper Class'.

As a wartime measure, the house and part of the estate at Caversham Park were taken over in 1943 by the BBC Overseas Monitoring Service. The rows of desks that once filled the rooms were replaced by banks of radio receivers manned by skilled operators of all nationalities, maintaining a listening watch day and night on radio transmissions from all parts of the world. Analysis of the information gleaned at Caversham proved vital for the conduct of the war.

The Central Hall in use as the Map Room, 1945. Here, detailed and up-to-date maps of all the theatres of war are available to those members of the staff who interpret the information received in the Listening Room for onward transmission to the appropriate departments. Although Caversham Park Village today occupies much of the parkland, the house continues to be used by the BBC. The service it provides remains a vital element in the process of news gathering.

The Newsroom, Radio 210, in the early days. Foreground, left to right: Kate Butler, Bob Morrison, Phil Coope (Head of News). Background: Graham Ledger, Mike Quinn. Reading's local commercial radio station, which first came on the air in March 1972, prides itself on the quality of its news broadcasts.

Radio 210 reports. The Prime Minister, Margaret Thatcher, talks to Phil Coope during a visit to the studio at Calcot.

Three

Transport

Rush hour, 1910. Pedestrians, cyclists, a horse-drawn cab and a Corporation tram throng King's Road at the end of a working day.

A Thames barge unloading timber at Caversham Bridge, 1865. Although by the middle of the nineteenth century the railways had captured much of the trade of the waterways, the carriage by water of heavy and bulky loads was still cheaper. The wide Thames barge with its shallow draught was the ideal craft for this purpose, and was used to carry timber from London docks to Reading until well into the twentieth century.

Volunteers of the Kennet & Avon Canal Trust engaged in dredging work at County Lock in the mid-1960s. The now-demolished maltings of the Courage Brewery are in the background. Founded in 1963, the trust has embarked with enthusiasm and success on the task of restoring and fully opening the canal through to Bath.

The ubiquitous horse, *c.* 1890. In spite of the coming of the railways, the development of steam power for road haulage and the arrival of the internal combustion engine, the horse continued to be the most common means of motive power for transporting people and goods. Here a team of four harnessed to a heavy cart, and a pair of horses in tandem, feed from their nosebags outside the Four Horseshoes, Basingstoke Road, while their drivers take their refreshment within.

Captain and Trixie, the last of Simonds' shire-horses to remain in active service. Once a familiar sight in Reading's streets, the heavy horses were replaced by motor vehicles at an early date. A few pairs were, however, retained as much for their publicity value as for their usefulness on the road.

Working in partnership, 1945. Fuel shortages during the Second World War brought horses back to the land. At Church Farm, Lower Basildon, a team of farm workers, including five girls of the Women's Land Army, work with a pair of heavy horses and a Massey-Harris tractor at the heavy but essential work of 'muck-spreading'.

A single-deck tram of the Reading Tramways Company, 1895. The privately owned company which was established in 1879 operated a single route from Brock Barracks via Broad Street and King's Road to Cemetery Junction. The depot and stables were in Oxford Road a short distance to the east of the railway bridge. The poor condition of the horses regularly attracted complaints and censure from the public. The company was taken over by the Corporation in 1901 and the horses were sold when electric trams were introduced in 1903.

The tramways depot and power station, Mill Lane. These buildings, together with the adjacent tram sheds, workshops and offices, occupied the site of the former St Giles Mill. The power for the system was provided by four compound steam engines, each driving a 100 kilowatt dynamo. The 150 ft chimney was demolished in 1938.

The Corporation's new trams came into service in July 1903. They offered a clean, fast and frequent service between The Pond House in Oxford Road and Palmer Park, and from Caversham Bridge to Whitley, with branches to Bath Road and Erleigh Road. The double-decker cars with seats for fifty had open tops to allow them to pass under the low bridges in Oxford Road and Caversham Road.

Opposite below: The electric tram was regarded at the turn of the century as the most up-to-date means of transport. The relaying of the tracks through the centre of Reading caused considerable disruption, but inconvenience was kept to a minimum by the employment of a large workforce and the use of prefabricated track sections. Electrification was accomplished in a very short space of time during the early months of 1903.

When trolleybuses replaced the trams, the last of which ran in May 1939, a new depot was built in Mill Lane. Temporary tracks were laid in this building to accommodate the last few trams in service.

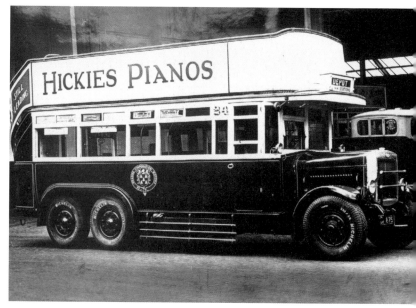

A maroon and cream giant of the road. The first motor buses were introduced in 1919. Four of these Guy six-wheelers with bodywork built in the Corporation's own workshops entered service in 1927. Seating fifty-four passengers they were to lead to the gradual replacement of the trams.

Dignity ... Two heavy lorries, laden with bales of straw ready for delivery outside the premises of Messrs Toomer, hay and straw merchants, in Friar Street, 1945.

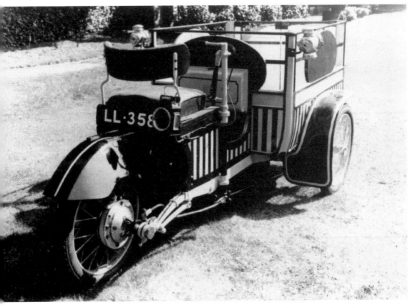

... and impudence. A motorized delivery tricycle of 1914 by Warrick of Caversham Road. Among its many unusual features is the steering tiller with integral gear selector and gearbox incorporated in the rear hub.

Reading General station, *c.* 1890. Built in the 1860s to replace Brunel's original wooden station, this building in Bath stone lent a certain dignity to what was hitherto a rather depressing part of the town.

The Great Western Hotel, opened in 1844 to serve travellers arriving by train. By this time the travelling public had transferred almost all of their custom from the roads, with the result that coach proprietors and innkeepers suffered great hardship.

The South Eastern Railway which linked Reading with Guildford and with its London terminus at Waterloo had its own station at Reading. Dating from 1860, this was a comparatively modest structure. The station closed in September 1965, since when its trains have run from the adjacent main-line station. The buildings, which served for a while as a service station, were finally demolished in 1982. The Apex Plaza now occupies the site.

Southern station a few days before its closure in September 1965. The notice by the barrier gives particulars of the revised arrangements.

A special train hauled by a Great Western 4-4-0 express locomotive of the 'Bulldog' Class about to depart from Reading station, 1899. The train was chartered for a day excursion by the Reading PSA (Pleasant Sunday Afternoon) Society, a non-conformist organization for adults whose motto, 'Brief, Bright and Brotherly', amply illustrates its approach to religious teaching.

Routes from Reading to the South-west. An ex-LSWR Class 'L11' 4-4-0 and an unidentified G.W. Churchward mogul engine stand in the west bay platforms with trains for Basingstoke and Newbury.

The main line to the west, 1946. A view from the former Reading main west signal box of the marshalling yards to the west of the town. Reading was at this time second only to Paddington as the busiest station on the line.

The trains of the Great Western Railway originally ran on tracks of 7 ft gauge. This was out of step with the other British main-line railways and in 1892 the system was converted to the nationally accepted standard gauge of 4 ft 8 ½ in. The last broad-gauge trains passed through Reading in May of that year.

A home on the move, 1934. Heelas' Removals Department did not confine itself to work in and around Reading. Here a container is loaded at Southampton for shipment to Canada.

Safe arrival. The Heelas container, having arrived safely in Vancouver, is towed to its final destination.

Four

Education

Children of St John's Church of England School, 1909.

Children's Christmas party, Holybrook Day Nursery, 1946. In the centre of the group is the matron, Mrs Maud Morris. Seated on the left is the housekeeper, Mrs Price. Seated on the right is Sister Daisy Beard. Mr Morris appears in the guise of Father Christmas. Provided by the local authority, day nurseries offered good, all-day care to the children of working mothers.

Nurses at Holybrook Day Nursery, 1946. Left to right: Mary Drinkwater, Evelyn ?, Ruby Hardy, Dorothy Tippings, Brenda Franklin, Mary Dray, Rosemary ?. In the background is one of the brick-built surface air-raid shelters provided at all Reading schools in the early stages of the Second World War. While not insurance against a direct hit, they at least offered protection from debris and the effects of blast.

Younger pupils of New Town School, 1938. Then, as now, the school served children from the densely populated area within the triangle bounded by London Road, the railway and the Kennet. Many were children of employees of Huntley & Palmers.

A junior stage presentation at George Palmer School, 1960.

Road safety education, 1934. As the amount of traffic on local roads increased, the teaching of road safety to young children became of vital importance. Learning through play, the children of Battle Infants School are busy with paste and paper building up their own road system.

Battle Mixed School, 1934. Handicrafts which could be used profitably in later life received a high priority in the school curriculum. A class of thirty of the older girls are engaged in lace making, embroidery and machine sewing.

Reading School, 1910. Of Reading's many schools, the oldest by far is Reading School. Originally situated in the Forbury, the school transferred to its present site in 1870 when the new buildings, built to the designs of Alfred Waterhouse, were formally opened by the Prince of Wales, the future King Edward VII.

Boys of the Reading Blue Coat School, 1911. The school, the name of which is derived from the distinctive uniform worn by its pupils, also has a long history. It was established in 1660 and endowed by Richard Aldworth, a Reading man who made his fortune as a London clothier. The school, now at Holme Park, Sonning, continues to thrive.

The Abbey School, established in 1887, was until 1913 known as Reading High School for Girls. The school was originally situated at No. 106 London Road, now the premises of the Gladstone Club.

The Abbey School teaching staff, 1906. Seated at the table is the headmistress, Miss H. Musson; to her left is her sister, Mary, who supervised the school's boarding house.

Above: In 1905 the school moved to its present location in Kendrick Road. The change of name to the Abbey School came in 1913 and recalls the school in the Abbey Gateway at which Jane Austen and Mrs Sherwood were once pupils.

Right: Commemoration Day, 1950. The Abbey School girls in best uniform with hats and gloves assemble prior to making their way to St Giles church for the annual commemoration service, an important day in the school year.

An inter-house tennis tournament in the late 1930s. The matches are being played on well-prepared lawns in front of the new wing, opened in 1927.

A science class in the Abbey School's well-equipped laboratory.

Marlborough House School. This was a preparatory school for boys originally situated on the south side of Bath Road, later transferring to larger premises in Parkside Road.

The Marlborough House School playing fields were situated on the opposite side of Parkside Road. In public school tradition, great importance was placed on games: cricket in summer and rugby in the winter. Since the Second World War these grounds have given way to housing.

Wilton House School, 1904. This was a purpose-built private school for girls in three acres of grounds. The prospectus offered 'a spacious schoolroom and dining hall, recreation room, airy classrooms and Swedish gymnasium', and stated that 'the sanitary arrangements and ventilation are on the newest and most approved systems'.

The dining hall at Wilton House School, 1909. The formal manner in which the tables are laid, the starched and folded napkins and the vases of plants on the tables all point to etiquette and the social graces being regarded as an integral part of the girls' education.

Leighton Park School. Established in 1890 by the Society of Friends, the school provided a public school type of education for boys. The original school house here was a square, brick building set in forty-five acres of parkland.

Leighton Park School, Reading. — Library

The library at Leighton Park School. This is an early view of the functional yet still imposing interior of the school.

University College, Reading. Established in 1892 under the auspices of Christ Church, Oxford, the University Extension College began life in a range of buildings in Valpy Street. It moved in 1906 to premises in London Road, a gift of the Palmer family. In 1926 the college was granted its formal charter of independence and became the University of Reading.

The Cloisters of the University College, 1910. The new college with its hall, quadrangle and cloisters, although of modern design, was built in such a way as to create an atmosphere redolent of traditional seats of learning.

Five

Local Events

The coronation of Her Majesty Queen Elizabeth II. A decorated float in the coronation procession, 2 June 1953.

Spectators and workmen view the remains of the inner gateway of the Abbey which, through long neglect, collapsed into the street during a stormy night in 1861.

The Abbey Gateway restored. So that the last recognizable fragment of the Abbey should not be lost for ever to the town, the ruined gateway was sensitively restored in 1862 by the architect Sir Gilbert Scott. It has since been used as a public meeting room.

In what are reputed to have been the worst floods for fifty years the Thames burst its banks in 1894. Much damage and distress was caused in the lower lying areas of Reading and Caversham. There was, however, no shortage of curious spectators willing to pay to take the 'water drive' in horse-drawn carts along Gosbrook Road to see the devastation.

Serious flooding in west Reading followed a torrential downpour on 9 June 1910. Oxford Road from Russell Street to The Pond House was for a time impassable. Here the whole length of Beresford Road from the junction with Oxford Road to Battle Farm is under water, the drainage system being quite unable to cope.

The Thames in flood, March 1947. A sudden thaw caused the river to rise by 15 inches overnight, causing the worst floods for half a century. Areas either side of the river from Lower Caversham to Great Knollys Street were affected.

Business as usual in the flooded market. A Dairy Shorthorn is led from the flooded pens to the auction which was held outside in the street.

Fire at the Little Miss Muffet factory, London Street, 6 July 1944. Here a fire in a packing material store created much smoke and confusion. There were, however, no injuries. The pipe running beside the pavement is an emergency water main for fire-fighting in case of air raids.

Fire at Waring & Gillow's furniture store, Friar Street, 14 February 1969. A ferocious blaze broke out during the busy lunch hour. Firemen are pouring water into the upper floors. Although there were more than fifty people in the shop at the time, all were evacuated without injury.

Broad Street decorated with the flags of all nations for the coronation of Edward VII,
1902. Bunting is strung from the posts which will shortly support the electric wires for the
Corporation's new trams.

Children and parents of Coventry Road, Newtown, many wearing souvenir medals celebrate the
coronation of King George VI, May 1937. Patriotic red, white and blue are much in evidence.

HRH The Prince of Wales, later King Edward VIII, paid a formal visit to Reading on 25 June 1926. After unveiling a commemorative plaque on Caversham Bridge, his crowded itinerary included a short journey by launch along the river.

No visitor to Reading should miss Huntley & Palmers. Having toured the factory, the prince, in the leading car, raises his hat to the crowd as the motorcade moves on to visit the Royal Berkshire Hospital and the university.

Coronation Day, 2 June 1953. The weather, ever fickle on festive occasions, was at its worst on the day of the Queen's coronation. The day was cold, and heavy rain fell during the late evening causing the cancellation of the open-air dancing at Thames Side Promenade. By 11 p.m. the centre of the town, although floodlit, was all but deserted.

The Freedom of the Borough, an honour rarely given, is bestowed upon Alderman Charles Gyningham Field, Mayor of Reading 1912–14, upon his retirement in 1935 from public affairs.

HRH Prince Arthur of Connaught is congratulated by the mayor upon his election in 1936 as High Steward of Reading. The ancient office of High Steward which ranks next in precedence after the mayor and the Recorder of the Borough, involves practically no duties and carries no emoluments yet is one of great dignity and some influence.

The Assize Courts, the Forbury. A view of the main courtroom from the public gallery. Bitter rivalry during the nineteenth century between Reading and Abingdon, for recognition as the County Town of Berkshire, was a spur to the building in Reading of the Assize Courts. Built at a cost of £21,644 3s 10d, the building housed the County Assizes and Quarter Sessions, the Reading County Petty Sessions and the headquarters of the recently formed Berkshire Constabulary. The Assizes sat here from 1861 until the establishment of the Crown Courts in 1972. The building remains, but the interior has been stripped in readiness for rebuilding at some as yet unspecified date to form part of the proposed Crown Courts complex.

The Judge's coach, 1899. From earliest times the Judges of Assize as direct representatives of the Sovereign have been received with full ceremonial. A coach with a liveried coachman and postillions supplied by the High Sheriff stands at the entrance to the Courts. The Under-Sheriff with his wand and two scarlet-coated trumpeters pose for the camera while waiting for the Judge to complete the day's business.

Within the ruined Abbey Chapter House, plaques on the far wall commemorate Hugh de Boves and Hugh Cook Faringdon, the first and last Abbots of Reading. To the left, unveiled in 1913 and in pristine condition, is a tablet presenting in facsimile the song, 'Sumer is icumen in'. The song is said to have been written in about 1240 by a monk at the Abbey.

A royal burial commemorated, 18 June 1921. To mark the 800th anniversary of the founding of Reading Abbey by King Henry I, a commemorative plaque near to the spot where the king is believed to be buried is unveiled by the Dean of Winchester.

The Maiwand Lion. Measuring 31 ft from nose to tail, this bronze lion commemorates the 328 officers and men of the Royal Berkshire Regiment who fell at Maiwand on 27 July 1880 during the Second Afghan Campaign.

Unable to withstand the ravages of the weather, the original terracotta plinth upon which the lion was mounted was replaced in 1911 by one of stone. The names of those who died at Maiwand are recorded on bronze tablets.

The ex-servicemen of the Veterans Association march through St Mary's Butts for their annual parade, August 1912. Parades and processions of all kinds, with their colour, music and movement, were guaranteed to attract crowds of spectators during the early years of the twentieth century.

Ready for inspection by General Sir Mowbray Thompson. Among the old soldiers on parade, two in the front rank wear campaign medals from the Crimean War.

The Distinguished Conduct Medal is presented at a parade in the Market Place, August 1917 to local soldier Sergeant A.H. Wigmore of the 2nd Battalion, KRRC. The citation stated that the sergeant, although twice wounded, brought eight comrades to safety while under heavy fire. The presentation was made by Major General W.G.W. Weston CB, who also presented the Military Medal to several other soldiers from the county.

Industrial unrest, 1919. The sense of euphoria that followed the end of the First World War was short lived. Due to a combination of economic factors aggravated by apparent lack of action on the part of an unimaginative government, many workers found their wages being cut at a time of rising prices. Many employers took the view that the time had come for a counterattack on inflated wartime wage rates. The result was a period of widespread industrial unrest. Bakery workers felt particularly hard-hit, since they were not to receive any addition to their wages for working the nightshift. As a result they withdrew their labour.

Queuing for bread at Swansea Road School. The shortage of bread was to cause hardship, particularly to the less well-off. To help ease the situation a number of local master bakers continued to produce such bread as they could. To achieve as fair a distribution as possible it was arranged that the bread would be made available at several local schools.

Members of the British Medical Aid Unit at the XIV International Brigade base hospital at Torreledones, during the Civil War in Spain, 1937. Reg Poole (middle row, left, sitting) and Nurse Thora Silverthorne (front row, right) were from Reading. Of the small group of men and women from Reading who fought with the International Brigades, five were to lose their lives.

Mobile blood transfusion unit and laboratory, 1937. Dr Reg Saxton from Reading and his driver are busy camouflaging their vehicle after crossing the Ebro. The doctor, whose pioneering work in blood transfusion helped save many lives in Spain, was later able to advise on the setting up of the blood transfusion service in Britain.

Fire Guards on duty on the roof of Reading Town Hall. Civic Defence regulations, which came into effect in 1939, required that no large premises were left unoccupied overnight in case of fire caused by enemy incendiary bombs. All members of staff were accordingly expected to take their turn at 'fire watching'.

The People's Pantry. Throughout the war the British Restaurants provided nutritious meals at a reasonable price to civilians and members of HM Forces alike. The People's Pantry in the Market Arcade was destroyed by a German Bomb on 10 February 1943, with a great loss of life and many people injured.

A wartime gift from the USA, 13 December 1940. An ambulance donated by twenty women of Reading, Pennsylvania, and allocated to Reading, Berkshire, is handed over by a representative of the Allied Relief Fund. The twenty Reading women pictured here were to act as 'Godmothers' to the ambulance and correspond with the American donors, informing them of the fate of the vehicle.

The mayor, Cllr William McIlroy, and deputy mayor, Alderman Alice Jenkins, together with the English ambulance driver read the plaque which carries the names of the donors.

The march on Aldermaston, 1958. Never before can Reading have seen anything like this protest march which, having commenced in Trafalgar Square on Good Friday, 4 April, deposited more than a thousand weary and footsore people in St Mary's Butts on Sunday evening. Supporters of the Campaign for Nuclear Disarmament, they were marching to the Atomic Weapons Research Establishment at Aldermaston not only to protest against the manufacture there of nuclear weapons, but to voice their general opposition to the alarming proliferation of nuclear arms. They reassembled on Easter Monday morning to complete the final leg of the journey. This was to become an annual pilgrimage for many years.

A noisy yet peaceful demonstration, 1977. When the lease of their club premises in Chain Street expired and they were left without a meeting place, members of the Central Youth Club, many of whom were of Afro-Caribbean origin, felt that their appeal to the Council for some alternative venue was being ignored. They made their feelings known by a noisy but good humoured protest march through the town centre.

Peaceful picketing. The young people also picketed a meeting of the County Council at Shire Hall to add weight to their request. Their efforts were rewarded and a new club premises in London Street made available to them.

Six

Sport and Leisure

A river trip to Goring aboard *River Queen*, Whitsun 1921.

Boys of the Alfred Sutton Boat Club about to compete in the Reading Amateur Regatta, 1965. The broad sweep of the Thames at Reading offers excellent water for rowing. The events that take place on this stretch of the river have, over the course of more than a century, attracted oarsmen from a wide area.

Younger members of Reading Swimming Club at the Arthur Hill Pool in the early 1950s. The baths remain in regular use, but since this time, redecoration and various improvements have greatly relieved the bare and rather spartan atmosphere.

Cycling at Palmer Park, 1952. Second in line is Jack Wicks who rode for Reading Wheelers from 1933 to 1940 and then as a member of the local Bon Amis Cycling Club. The cycle track dates from 1897. The shale surface was replaced with asphalt in 1955 and again improved in 1978.

De Havilland Moths lined up at a meeting of the Reading Aero Club, Woodley Aerodrome, in the mid-1930s. The club owed its existence to Charles Powis, a partner in the firm of Phillips & Powis, who, having so enjoyed his first flight a couple of years previously, decided that this was the sport for him. The very successful Reading Flying Club was formed in 1930.

A Reading motor cycle ace. This life-size marble figure in Reading Cemetery marks the last resting place of Bernard Laurence Hieatt. He died on 3 May 1930, aged twenty-one, in a tragic accident at Brooklands. Riding in bad weather in a 200 mile sidecar race, he was leading by a handsome margin when he touched the grass bank at the side of the track and overturned. He was killed instantly. At earlier events at the same meeting he had broken world records in a 1,000 mile sidecar race and in a two-hour event. Bernard Hieatt's interests also extended to aviation. A member of Reading Aero Club, he would often fly in his yellow biplane to tracks where he was to ride.

Reading Golf Club with its course at Emmer Green was established in 1910. Until the early 1960s one of the club's major trophies was the President's Putter, here being presented in 1950 by the president, Mr R.W. Neale.

Exhibition march between well-known professional golfers, Pat Roberts and John Panton, 1954.

Tournament winners, 1963. The couple holding the Reading Mercury Open Foursomes Cup are Bertie and Mona Fortescue. Mr Fortescue has been a member of the club for over seventy years and is still going strong.

Disaster struck in June 1963 when a serious fire destroyed the clubhouse. Before long a new building arose from the ashes.

The Abbey Rugby Football Club, 1962. The captain, P. Gaines, is holding the ball. The club was formed in 1956 from members then too old to continue in the Youth League fixtures. It was for some years without a home of its own, but has since 1970 developed an excellent clubhouse and grounds at Emmer Green.

The Abbey team in action at Aldermaston playing Newbury in the Berkshire Cup.

Temperance League Football Club, 1895/6. Amateur football became immensely popular towards the end of the nineteenth century. Clubs, churches and schools all turned out teams that played regularly in a variety of local leagues. The Reading Temperance Society's team in the Temperance League was particularly strong.

The Temperance League team, 1903/4 season.

The Biscuitmen, Reading Football Club, 1911/12. Following a couple of disappointing seasons, a revitalized team fought its way to the top of the Second Division of the Southern League and were runners-up in that year's FA Cup competition. Trainer Billy Beats (in the cap) is standing to the left of the group.

Reading Football Club, 1924. Football was suspended during the First World War but soon returned with renewed vigour. Reading were now in the Football League Division Three and went on to become champions in 1925/6. The captain is Bert Eggo (centre).

Hospital Radio Reading came into the world in September 1957. It was the result of an idea conceived by Les Warth while himself a patient in hospital. With the co-operation of Reading Football Club, borrowed army equipment was used to relay live commentary by Maurice Edelstone, of a 3-0 victory to Reading Royals over Aldershot, to receivers in Battle Hospital.

Les Warth at the console, 1976. Having outgrown its accommodation at Elm Park and with the assistance and co-operation of the Local Health Authority, the service moved into a new studio complex at Battle Hospital. From there it continues to offer a full programme of sports coverage, local news, patients' requests and live shows direct from the Hexagon.

A parade of civilian and service organizations, possibly marking 'Wings for Victory' week, 1941. Berkshire nurses taking part march past the saluting base in St Mary's Butts.

The next generation of nurses, 1944. Members of the Junior Red Cross (Berkshire 5,000) are outside St Lawrence's Hall.

Red Cross week, May 1965. Acknowledging their service to the community, the Mayor of Reading, Mrs Alexandra Sturrock, makes her donation to two Red Cross youth members collecting outside Heelas, Broad Street.

The Girls Brigade, 1959. Leaders and members of the Wesley church smartly turned out at their parents' evening. Brother and sister organizations, the Boys and Girls Brigades, have from their earliest days had a strong following in Reading.

Sea Scouts attending the King's Road Baptist church for Church Parade, 1947. The little boy walking with his father seems to be saying that he, too, would like to be a Scout one day.

Y.W.C.A. READING. 104.

A social centre for working girls. The YWCA Girls' Institute and Boarding House, Devonshire House, No. 19 Castle Street. In its earlier years the Reading branch of the YWCA, an interdenominational movement 'for the uniting of women of various business establishments', met twice weekly at a house in St Mary's churchyard. By 1882 a hostel offering both a meeting place and residential accommodation for young working women, many of whom were employed in the larger local shops, had been established.

William Isaac Palmer, a partner in the family firm from 1857 until his death in 1893, was a strong believer in the virtues of abstinence and actively involved in the Temperance Movement, both locally and nationally. He promoted the Blue Ribbon movement in the town, was a founder of the local Help Myself Society and, from 1870, was President of the Reading Temperance Society.

The Temperance Society obtained premises of its own in 1862 in the former Working Men's Club in West Street. It could now offer a venue for food, non-alcoholic drink and companionship. There were also a reading room and a free library, the books from which were later to be added to those of the new Municipal Library. The society did not just aim to stop drinking, but was really an argument as to how leisure should properly be spent.

137

Left: As a memorial to W.I. Palmer, the West Street Temperance Society premises were enlarged in 1899 to form the Palmer Memorial Buildings. The ornamental gateway was executed by the architect Slingsby Stallwood.

Below: West Street Hall. This large hall formed part of the Memorial Building. Although used primarily for Temperance events, it was also a popular venue for meetings, concerts and other functions compatible with the aims of the Temperance Society.

The Reading Temperance Prize Band, 1906. The band owed its formation to William Palmer who, in 1851, presented the first set of instruments. With a repertoire of martial and concert music, the band in its smart uniform was very much in demand for parades and processions. The band also performed regularly in the Forbury Gardens.

The Temperance Queen, 1955. Elected annually, the Temperance Queen played a leading role in the social activities of the society. Her coronation was invariably a glittering and happy occasion.

The Queen's Hall Assembly Rooms, Valpy Street, 1890. Built by Robert Tompkins, proprietor of a horse and carriage repository in Merchants Place, the hall offered a conveniently situated venue for both serious gatherings and light entertainment.

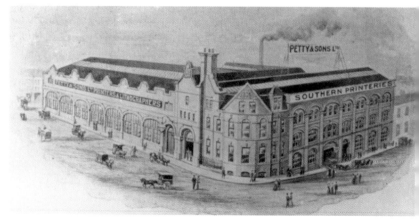

A change of use for the Queen's Hall. Following Robert Tompkins' death in 1897 at the age of 63, his estate was sold. There being no buyer for the hall as a going concern, it was converted by Messrs Petty & Sons, lithographers and printers, to a printing works and warehouse.

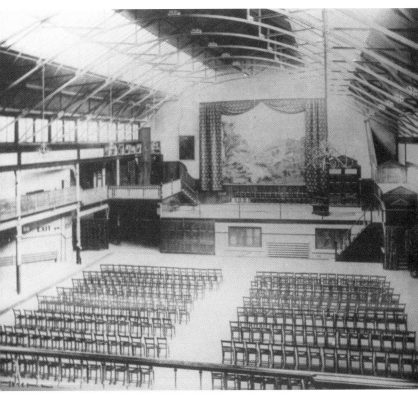

The Queen's Hall, 1890s. In contrast to its rather forbidding exterior, the hall was exceptionally well appointed. It rivalled the then new Town Hall both in size and in the facilities it offered. Ironically the grandest functions to be held in the hall, a reception in honour of the Prince of Wales following a visit to the University Extension College, and a Conservative and Unionist Party Conference, took place only a few days prior to the sale of the hall.

Reading Amateur Radio Club direction-finding exercise, 1949. The radio 'Ham' does not spend all of his time in the 'shack' crouched over his set. Using equipment mainly built by themselves, the members of the Reading Club take part in a direction-finding exercise at Mortimer Common.

Hamfest, 1951. A high spot in the Reading Amateur Radio Club's year was the annual reunion and celebration, known to the members as the Hamfest, at which prizes and trophies were presented. The earlier meetings took place in the new People's Pantry in Cross Street, now the site of Marks & Spencers.

The Reading Amateur Radio Club, 1947. With the end of the war, amateur radio enthusiasts were free once again to contact fellow operators across the world. At a club open day the mayor, Mrs Phoebe Cusden, sees an amateur radio station in operation. The cards on the wall behind the equipment confirm successful contacts.

Reading & District Philatelic Society's annual exhibition, c. 1955. Members' stamp collections on display attract considerable interest.

A scene from *A Winter's Tale*, the Progress Theatre, 1963. The theatre, which was formed in the early post-war years, was able in 1951 to secure premises of its own at The Mount, Christchurch Road. From small beginnings this enthusiastic company has brought the pleasure of live theatre to people wishing to take part not only as performers but in all the other aspects of theatrical work. An active student group has also helped introduce young people to the magic of the theatre.

A period piece at the Progress Theatre, 1963. This scene from *The Beaux' Stratagem* indicates a quality of setting and costume rivalling those of many a professional company.

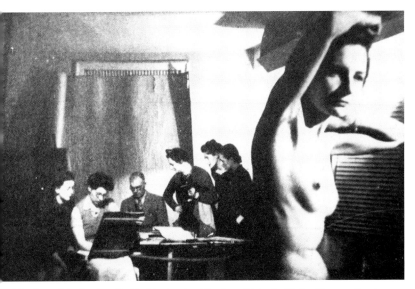

Members of the Reading Guild of Artists sketching from life in the Market Place studio of Gilbert Adams, 1944. Founded in 1930, the guild continues to encourage the exhibition by its members of serious works of art.

Shove ha'penny at the Trades Union Club, Minster Street, 1946. Then, as now, the club served as a social centre for the working man, a place to go for advice concerning employment and welfare matters, and a handy venue for meetings. Recently the club has transferred to purpose-built premises in Chatham Street.

Caversham Lock, 1907. The quiet sport of angling has long been one of the pleasures of the river. Here an elderly gentleman casts his line into waters which are as yet relatively unpolluted, despite the factories further upstream.

Prospect Park, 1914. The park provided a public open space for the west of Reading with recreational facilities including football pitches, a bowling green and tennis courts. The grass was left uncut between the end of the football season and haymaking and areas were occasionally fenced off to provide grazing for sheep.

The Forbury Gardens. For centuries, this was little more than an area of rough ground where fairs and cattle markets were held. The Forbury was acquired by the Reading Board of Health in 1862 and laid out as formal public gardens, a pleasant place in which to walk or sit.

The Thames Side Promenade to the west of Caversham Bridge was opened as a public space in 1910. It owes its existence to labour activist Lorenzo Quelch, who managed to persuade members of the Council that there was much to be gained by providing the local unemployed with work which would help enable the people of Reading to enjoy the town's greatest asset— its river.

River steamer *Britannia* on an excursion from Windsor, moored at the Promenade near Caversham Bridge while her passengers spend time ashore, 1925. Reading was a popular destination for river trips from other towns along the Thames.

A striking and unusual craft, the training brig *King Alfred*. Christened by Lady Rose of Hardwick on Trafalgar Day 1909, to train boys of naval-oriented organizations, the brig was a feature of the river until her departure in 1919.

St Peter's church, Caversham, and the Old Rectory provide the backdrop to this peaceful river scene, 1925. The two skiffs, each with seats for three and easily handled by a single oarsman, could be hired by the hour from the many boatyards around Caversham Bridge and were very much in demand by visitors.

Boats for hire. From the end of the last century until the First World War, boating was at its most popular. Throughout the summer months the river was crowded with small craft. The river bank between Caversham Bridge and Caversham Lock was particularly well supplied with landing stages where boats could be hired.

Kennet Mouth, the point at which the Kennet flows into the Thames, c. 1910. A neat steam launch lies moored at the landing stage, while two young ladies take to the water in a skiff hired from Mr Wheeler. From this point it was possible to make one's way along the Thames or into the somewhat less attractive lower reaches of the Kennet.

The Roebuck, c. 1900. This inn, with its views across the river into Oxfordshire, was popular as a mooring place for small craft and a haven for fishermen. Access to the inn from the river bank was by way of a footbridge across the railway.

The White Hart, Sonning, 1908. This was a popular destination both for walkers from Reading and for those wishing to enjoy a short trip on the river without having to pass through locks. Painted on the steps of the landing stage of the White Hart is 'Landing stage for launches of any draught'.

Heelas staff outing, June 1926. The managers and staff of Heelas department store pose for photographs before setting off in a variety of cars and charabancs on an outing to the British Empire Exhibition at Wembley. On the far left at the junction of Chain Street and Minster Street is the antique furniture business owned by the father of the late Arthur Negus, the well-known authority and broadcaster on antiques. Could that be young Arthur himself observing the scene from the first-floor window?

The single screw steamer *Fashion*, possibly on her maiden voyage, 1887. The vessel, built in this year for Mr Antonio Bona, proprietor of the Caversham Bridge Hotel, casts off from the landing stage with a full complement of fashionably dressed passengers.

Mapledurham Mill, 1910. This picturesque old mill with its two waterwheels invariably attracted the interest of passengers on the passing pleasure boats, and was a favourite subject for artists.

A women's group from Elm Park Hall set off from Cranbury Road on a day's outing in the 1920s. At this time, when for a great many people travel for pleasure was a rare treat, the open-top charabanc, despite its scant shelter in inclement weather, was the ideal vehicle from which to view the countryside.

Theale.   *near Reading.*

Theale at the turn of the century. A sleepy village on the road from Reading and the last port of call before the town for thirsty tourists.

Pangbourne, *c.* 1900. Only five miles from Reading and still truly rural, the village of Pangbourne attracted visitors both from Reading and from further afield.

Shooters Hill, Pangbourne.

Shooters Hill on the riverside road from Pangbourne to Streatley, leading to an as yet unspoiled stretch of the Thames, was popular with boating and fishing parties.

Across the Thames from Pangbourne, the Oxfordshire village of Whitchurch in the early 1930s. The Greyhound Inn, on the right, was favoured by charabanc drivers taking passengers from Reading on sightseeing tours or for an evening mystery trip.

Sonning village, a destination popular with Reading people. Not only was this very attractive village readily accessible by river, there being no locks to be negotiated between Caversham and Sonning, but it could also be reached on foot, a gentle afternoon's walk, by way of the Thames towpath.

Gilbert Ernest Child-Beale (1868–1967), gentleman farmer and keen yachtsman, in typical
pose. In 1956, with a vision of preserving a beautiful area of the Thames Valley in perpetuity for
public enjoyment and relaxation, he created a charitable trust dedicating an area of his land at
Lower Basildon as a park open to the public where visitors might enjoy the scenery, picnic and
see the peacocks that roamed the site. He also provided two boats to take visitors on short trips
along the river. Still known locally as The Peacock Farm, the Child-Beale Bird Park at Basildon
near Pangbourne has since 1956 proved a unique attraction. In recent years the grounds have
been greatly enlarged and many attractions, including ornamental waterfowl and rare breeds of
livestock, children's play areas, café and shop, have been added.

The Pavilion, Child-Beale Park. This fanciful structure, surrounded by an assortment of amusing statuary, was designed and built by Gilbert Beale himself in 1955 as a memorial to his parents. Here at the heart of the park which he had created he would in observing the visitors share in their enjoyment. Today this building houses the National Model Ship and Boat Exhibition Centre.

The retirement of the *Swan of Basildon*. After twenty years of service, during which time she carried no less than 186,000 passengers completely without charge, this boat had earned a rest. Two huge mobile cranes lift her from the water to the bank where, for a little longer, she was to rest as a feature in the children's play area.

Fans in their thousands flocked in 1971 to the National Jazz, Blues and Rock Festival, which took place in the area between Richfield Avenue and the Thames Side Promenade, now occupied by the sports centre. This gathering, which began in the early 1960s as a jazz festival in Richmond Park and moved to Reading in 1971 as the National Jazz, Blues and Rock Festival, occupies three days every August Bank Holiday attracting tens of thousands of mainly young people. Beyond the boundary fences of the festival site with its enormous open-air arena is an unplanned, temporary canvas city of tents and caravans.

Acknowledgements

I would like to thank all those who have helped me compile this collection of photographs. A number of the old photographs in this book are drawn from the Illustrations Collection in the Berkshire County Local Studies Library and are reproduced by kind permission of the County Librarian. With apologies for any inadvertent omissions I must acknowledge with thanks the many friends and organizations that have contributed material and advice and especially mention the following:

Mrs Molly Casey; Mr and Mrs P.G. Dray; Mr Ron Eames; Mr J.K. Major; Mr John Mauger; Mr Bob Nash; Ms E. O'Keefe; Ms Mairead Panetta; Mr Ron Pugsley; Mr David Quartermaine; Dr R.S. Saxton; Miss B.C.L. Sheldon; Dr C.F. Slade; Mrs Margaret Smith; Mrs Jill Toft; Capt. Les Warth; Mr L. Wicks; the Abbey RFC; the Abbey School; Amethyst Centre for Alcohol Concern; Museum of English Rural Life; Berkshire Youth & Community Service; British Broadcasting Corporation; British Red Cross; Brookfield Shires plc; The Child-Beale Wildlife Trust; Hospital Radio Reading; Lens of Sutton; Marx Memorial Library (International Brigade Archive); National Motor Museum, Beaulieu; The Progress Theatre; Radio 210; Reading Amateur Radio Club; The Reading Guild of Artists; Reading Newspaper Co. Ltd; Reading Schools Rowing Association; Reading Swimming Club; Royal Berkshire Aviation Society; Messrs Thimbleby and Shorland; The Times Newspapers Ltd.

A very special word of thanks for Mr Peter Gibson of Cockett, Swansea, whose photographic wizardry has made possible the reproduction of many of the older and sometimes damaged photographs in this book. Finally, but by no means least, a special word of thanks to my wife, Mary, for her patience and encouragement.